What Do We Know About Fairies?

by Ben Hubbard

illustrated by Laurie A. Conley

Penguin Workshop

For Robin and Fizzy Pop: Brighton Clappers—BH

For Madeline and Violet—LAC

PENGUIN WORKSHOP
An imprint of Penguin Random House LLC
1745 Broadway, New York, NY 10019
penguinrandomhouse.com

Library of Congress Cataloging-in-Publication Data is available.

First published in the United States of America by Penguin Workshop, 2026

Manufactured in the United States of America
CJKW

ISBN 9798217141579 (paperback)
10 9 8 7 6 5 4 3 2 1

ISBN 9798217141586 (library binding)
10 9 8 7 6 5 4 3 2 1

The authorized representative in the EU for product safety and compliance is Penguin Random House Ireland, Morrison Chambers, 32 Nassau Street, Dublin D02 YH68, Ireland, https://eu-contact.penguin.ie.

Contents

What Do We Know About Fairies?

In 1917, the first ever photographs of fairies emerged from a small village in northern England. Sixteen-year-old Elsie Wright and her cousin, nine-year-old Frances Griffiths, had taken the pictures at the bottom of Elsie's garden, in Cottingley, West Yorkshire. The garden led to a quiet, secluded stream where the girls loved to play and explore. But they often came home dirty and wet, which annoyed Elsie's mother, Polly. What had made them so wet? The girls said it was the fairies that they had been playing with. This annoyed Elsie's father, Arthur. If there was such a thing as fairies, then perhaps the girls should take a photo of them, he said. So, the girls borrowed Arthur's camera and returned an hour later smiling triumphantly. They said they had taken a picture of a fairy.

Arthur developed the image in his home darkroom and was confused by what he saw. It showed Frances sitting behind a bush on which four female fairies were dancing. The fairies were a few inches high, wore short dresses, and had butterfly-type wings on their backs. One fairy appeared to be playing a clarinet. Arthur was far from convinced. He asked why there were "bits of paper" in the photo and treated it as a joke.

He reacted the same way when the girls took a similar photograph a few months later. This photo showed a slightly larger winged male who was dancing and touching Elsie's hand.

Although the girls insisted the images were genuine, Arthur did not believe them. But Polly did. She thought the images were real. She took them to a lecture on fairies that happened to be taking place in the nearby city of Bradford. The lecture was being held by the Theosophical (say: Thee-os-OFF-ick-kul) Society. Theosophists believe in spirits, supernatural beings, and mystical experiences that normally go unseen by people. The members were fascinated by Polly's photos and had them examined by photographer Harold Snelling. Snelling said they were "genuine unfaked photographs." This created something of a stir, as no photo of a fairy had ever been seen before. The Theosophical Society began a series of public lectures on the fairy photos soon afterward.

The pictures soon caught the attention of Arthur Conan Doyle, creator of Sherlock Holmes. By chance, Conan Doyle had been asked to write an article for *The Strand* magazine about whether fairies existed. The fairy photos seemed to have emerged at exactly the right moment. Conan Doyle asked an expert at the Kodak photographic company to check the photos. The expert said they had not been faked. Delighted, Conan Doyle published his article called "Fairies Photographed." He then asked Frances and Elsie to provide more photos of fairies. The girls took three more fairy photos. These showed fairies flying and hiding in the grass, and offering flowers to Elsie. Conan Doyle used these images for a second article about fairies. In the articles, Conan Doyle said that fairies did exist and that the photos proved this.

The articles were published in England, South Africa, and the United States, and caused a great sensation. Some people thought the photos were a hoax and that Frances and Elsie had made the whole thing up. But others were excited by the pictures and took them as proof that fairies existed. Many people, it seemed, believed in fairies. But who was right? Were the Cottingley fairy photos real? And do fairies actually exist? What do we really know about fairies?

CHAPTER 1
What Is a Fairy?

Arthur Conan Doyle's fame and reputation brought worldwide attention to the Cottingley fairy photos, and to fairies in general. Conan Doyle believed fairies existed and said the photos taken by Frances and Elsie provided the proof. Some people agreed with him. Others disputed the photos and said fairies did not exist. But still more people thought the photos were fake because fairies did not look or behave like the friendly winged females shown. They did, however, believe

Arthur Conan Doyle

in a different idea of fairies. In fact, many people in Britain had reported seeing fairies in their lifetimes. This number increased after Conan Doyle's articles came out. Suddenly, people wanted to describe their personal encounters with fairies.

In 1922, Conan Doyle published accounts of some of the other fairy encounters in a book called *The Coming of the Fairies*. In one account, Mrs. Tweedale of Devon described seeing a leaf moving strangely in her garden. This is what she saw:

"Expecting to see a field-mouse astride it, I stepped very softly up to it. What was my delight to see a tiny green man. He was about five inches long, and was swinging back-downwards. His tiny green feet, which appeared to be green-booted, were crossed over the leaf, and his hands, raised behind his head, also held the blade. I had a vision of a merry little face and something red in the form of a cap on the head. For a full minute he remained in view, swinging on the leaf. Then he vanished."

In another account, Yorkshire man Tom Tyrrell described seeing fairies several times in his local forest:

"They seem afraid of me, and they scamper off up the trees like squirrels . . . They are certainly like human beings, only very small, say about twelve or fifteen inches high . . . with fairly large heads and standing-up ears, out of proportion to the size of their bodies, and bandy legs." (Bandy legs curve outward at the knees and are also called "bowlegs.")

These two accounts are typical of how humans describe their encounters with fairies. In fact, people have reported seeing fairies for thousands of years. Some of these fairies are as small as ants, others as large as children. Some are wingless, dwell underground, and like to be left alone. Others live in the woods, waiting to play pranks on people walking past. Some fairies are friendly, kind, and helpful, and do chores in humans' homes.

Other fairies can be dangerous and harmful. Fairies have been said to kidnap people, cause damage and destruction in homes, and steal babies from their cribs.

Lutin fairy

There are believed to be many types of fairies around the world, with many different names. These include brownies, Lutins (say: LOO-tuns), Jogah (say: JOE-ga), Aziza (say: Az-SEES-a), Patupaiarehe (say: PAH-too-pie-ah-reh-heh), and more. But although there are many different fairies, there are also plenty of things that unite them. So what do fairies have in common?

Most fairies are believed to be mysterious,

magical beings with supernatural powers. They live in natural settings and are often the guardians and protectors of these places. Fairies can be found in forests, fields, forts, and on mountaintops. Some fairies are said to live in homes. There are also fairy realms: whole worlds that are close to ours, but invisible or hidden to humans.

Some people have entered these realms through special portals, but only a fairy can take people through. Fairy realms are described as sunny, green kingdoms, full of fun, feasting, and dancing—although time passes differently there. A few days in a fairy realm can be the same as several years on Earth.

Most fairies are described as small, usually ranging from one inch to around four feet tall. Some are light enough to walk along the leaves of a tree, but others are stout and solidly built. Fairies often wear clothes of green, brown, and red, and some have green eyes and hair. A few fairies have wings, but most are reported to be wingless. Fairies can appear and disappear at will, and sometimes take the form of animals.

Seeing a fairy is a rare and exciting event, but it does not always mean the fairy is happy to be found.

Some fairies, such as the Ainu Korpokkur (say: kor-POE-ker), don't like to be seen, and become angry if people look for them. The South American Duende (say: DOO-wend-day) hides in the walls of houses, and is only seen when it jumps out at children to scare them.

The Finnish Haltija (say: HALL-tee-a) is hardly ever seen at all, but it is known to be a kind fairy who protects forests, farms, and homes. Seeing the Scottish Redcap, on the other hand, almost always means trouble. The Redcap has long, thin arms, claws for fingers, fiery red eyes, and a cap that is bright red from being soaked in human blood.

It is wise not to upset a fairy, which is tricky as they are easily offended. Searching for fairies,

talking badly about them, and giving them the wrong gift can make them angry. Some fairies take only a simple bowl of milk in payment for their kind deeds and are insulted if offered anything more. Milk, cakes, and cream are favorite foods of fairies and they are said to follow a vegetarian diet. Those who have visited a fairy realm reported cider, wine, and honey were also served at their fairy feasts.

Korpokkur

The Korpokkur are fairies from northern Japan, home of the ancient Ainu people. According to the Ainu, the Korpokkur are so small that a whole family can fit under one burdock leaf. Korpokkur therefore means "the people who live under the burdock leaves." The Korpokkur are nimble, quick, and difficult to get a glimpse of. Long ago, the Korpokkur left fish outside humans' huts at night and the Ainu would leave gifts in return. But in one story, an Ainu man caught a female Korpokkur by the arm to look at her. This made the Korpokkur so angry that they went into hiding and are today more elusive than ever.

CHAPTER 2
The First Fairies

Belief in fairies is thousands of years old. Fairies are first mentioned in *The Iliad*, one of the world's oldest poems, written by Homer in around 700 BCE. *The Iliad* tells the story of the Trojan War, where Homer mentions "the nymphs who live forever." Nymphs were believed to be a type of female nature spirit with magical powers. They were strongly connected to trees, water, and other natural objects. They were also fond of music and dancing. They were, in other words, an early type of fairy.

Homer

A nymph called Calypso appears in Homer's poem *The Odyssey*. In *The Odyssey*, Calypso puts the shipwrecked hero Odysseus under a spell so she can keep him on her island. Just like later fairies who abduct humans, Calypso keeps Odysseus captive for many years before releasing him.

Nymphs were not the only fairies of the ancient world. In Persia, the peri were also a type of nature spirit. According to Persian folklore, peri were small winged females who glowed with a shimmering light. They did not need to eat but instead survived by smelling sweet flowers.

Like nymphs, the peri could abduct humans and take them to their own world. This might be a punishment for something humans had done wrong. But at other times, the peri were kind and helpful to people.

Not all ancient fairies were helpful and kind. The jinni of Arabic mythology could cause humans harm. Like later fairies, jinni would punish people for speaking badly about them, even if this was unintentional. The jinni could also take animal and human form and even inhabit non-moving objects, such as trees, rocks, and buildings. Travelers believed jinni lived in remote parts of the desert, where they could cause accidents or give people diseases.

In the Middle Ages, fairies were almost always connected to particular places. In Europe, they were said to dwell in hills, forts, and fairy rings. This was a time when people worked on the land and were superstitious about the world around them. Fairies were seen not as friendly and cute but as unpredictable creatures with magical powers that could cause harm. Extra caution was taken when passing by a fairy dwelling, such as a fairy ring.

A fairy ring is a circle of mushrooms or toadstools commonly found in the European countryside and on grassy lawns in the United States. Sometimes a circular area of moss or trampled grass is also called a fairy ring. People said fairies danced in the rings at night under the light of the moon. Just seeing this dancing could bring bad luck to a human, while joining in was even worse. Sometimes the fairies would beckon humans over to dance with them. But once inside the ring, the person would disappear to the fairy realm. Here, the fairies would make the person dance for days on end until they died from exhaustion. Others were returned home, only to find that many years had passed in their absence.

Even entering a ring at any time was unadvisable. Kicking over a mushroom in a fairy ring could bring a serious illness, accident,

or early death. There were also certain ways to avoid these fates. To prevent a fairy punishment, a person could run around a fairy ring nine times. They could also wear a hat backward, which was said to confuse the fairies. The simplest thing, on the other hand, was to just walk past a fairy ring and not disturb it. In parts of rural France today, people would never dream of setting foot inside a fairy ring.

In France in the Middle Ages, fairies were not only seen in fairy rings. The French fairies known as Dames Blanches were said to live in ravines, bridges, and river crossings in the provinces of Normandy and Lorraine. Here, the fairies would stop travelers and demand a dance before they could pass. If the traveler agreed, the Dames Blanches would bow and then disappear. But if the traveler refused, they would later suffer a misfortune.

Another French fairy, called a Lutin, could turn itself into a horse, fully saddled and ready to ride! But if a human mounted the horse, the Lutin would ride away with them to the fairy realm and never be seen again.

Just as in France, the fairies of Eastern Europe also sometimes appeared as animals, such as deer. The fairies of Croatia, Hungary, and Slovenia were also known to invite people to parties, like the nymphs of the ancient world.

The fairies would ride in on thunderstorms and play whistles, beat drums, and dance. Ordinary people could join these celebrations and the fairies would provide a feast. However, all was not as it seemed. After the people had eaten the fine foods on offer and ended their night with the fairies, they would find that they were still hungry. It had all been a fairy illusion.

What's in a Name?

The word *fairy* originated in France. In Old French, the words *fee*, *fey*, *fae*, and *faie* were used to describe an enchanted woman skilled in magic. The words came from the Latin word *fatum*, which means "to enchant." Over time, these words became *faerie* in English. During the Middle Ages, *faerie* became *fairy*. Today it is the common English word we use for the many differently named fairies around the world. They are also still referred to as the "fey" or "fae."

CHAPTER 3
Fairies of Britain and Ireland

During the Middle Ages, stories about fairies were part of the folklore of many different countries. Folklore focuses on the myths, legends, and folktales of a certain place. Folktales are stories usually handed down by word of mouth, which means that they were spoken out loud, told from generation to generation. But starting in the twelfth century (1100–1200 CE), authors in Britain and Ireland began traveling around these countries and writing their fairy folktales and encounters down. These authors were often priests, such as Ralph of Coggeshall and Gerald of Wales. Because these men could write, we know more about fairy folklore encounters in Britain and Ireland during the Middle Ages than anywhere else in the world.

One story described by Ralph of Coggeshall was about an invisible girl called Malekin. Malekin had emerged in Dagworthy Castle in Suffolk, England. She made contact with the castle's lord, his family, and their servants by talking to them. She said she had been abducted by fairies when she was a baby and now lived in the fairy realm. The castle's servants left food out for Malekin and got used to speaking with her.

Ralph of Coggeshall

Malekin once showed herself to a chambermaid (a bedroom servant) who said the girl looked about seven years old and wore a white dress. Malekin said she had spent seven years in captivity and had seven more to go. This was because the fairies had to release their captives after fourteen years.

The story is an early example of the commonly reported practice of fairies stealing babies. Fairies were said to take human babies when they did not have enough of their own to raise. In the baby's place, the fairies would leave a substitute called a changeling. A changeling could take many forms. Sometimes, it was a log of wood carved into the shape of a baby and brought to life under a fairy spell. At other times, the changeling was a small, hairy monster. A changeling could also be an elderly fairy with the body of a baby but an old, withered face. These changelings would cry, whine, and sob constantly. It was possible to trick the elderly fairies into revealing themselves, though. To do this, a mother would set twenty-four empty eggshells on the hearth (the floor of a fireplace) and pretend to start preparing a drink (which they called "brewing") in them.

The changeling would then cry out in a shrill voice: "I have seen the first acorn before the oak, but I have never seen brewing in eggshells before!" The mother would then throw the changeling into the fire, who would fly up the chimney laughing and shrieking. Afterward, the human baby who had been taken would appear at the front door of their own home, unharmed.

In Scotland, there were a few ways of stopping a baby from being replaced by a changeling. First, an expectant mother would keep her pregnancy secret for as long as possible. Then, she would leave metal objects near the cradle—knives, scissors, even nails—as fairies hated iron and would stay away. A father's clothes put in the crib would also scare fairies away. In one story from Selkirk, Scotland, a mother heard fairies laughing in the room next to the bedroom. Alarmed, the mother threw her husband's vest over her and her newborn child.

She then heard a scream from the fairies, who cried out, “Auld luck has cheated us o’ our bairnie [baby]!”

The fairies disappeared, but something then fell down the chimney. It was a wax model of a baby, which the fairies were going to use as a changeling substitute for the child.

Fairies were not always the foes of humans in these stories—they could also be friends. Sometimes, fairies would ask people for help and give them a great reward in return. In one such tale, a female fairy in a green costume asked a Scottish farmer's wife for some grain. In return for her kindness, the farmer's wife later received an everlasting meal that could never be finished.

Another famous type of fairy who helped farmers with their work was a brownie. Stories of brownies feature widely in the Scottish folklore: They are among the country's best-known fairies.

A brownie was usually described as a small man, around three feet high, dressed in ragged brown clothes. Brownies were said to live around a house or farm, where they performed chores such as separating grain, herding sheep, or sweeping floors. In return, a brownie was given a bowl of milk or cream, or sometimes a small cake. But there were strict rules about this payment, which had to be left out and never given directly to the brownie. Trying to reward a brownie with anything more, such as extra food or new clothes, was taken as a great insult. If a brownie became offended, he would either disappear or turn into a boggart. A boggart was a nasty fairy who would torment a family in their home. He would snatch away food, push children into corners and cupboards, and shake beds violently during the night. Boggarts were thought to be the model for a later supernatural spirit called a poltergeist.

Unfortunately, there was no remedy for living with a boggart, who would follow a family even if they moved to a new home.

In England, a mischievous fairy similar to a brownie was a puck. Pucks would live in human homes and help with housework—as long as no one annoyed them. In this way, a puck was similar to other European household fairies, such as the German kobold (say: KOE-bold), the Danish and Swedish tomte (say: TOM-ter), the Norwegian nisse (say: NEE-suh), and the Russian domovoy (say: DORM-o-voi).

Pucks were widely reported in England's Sussex and Worcestershire, and today these counties still have puck place-names, such as Puckscroft, Upper Puck Hill, and Puck Pit.

Encounters with pucks would usually follow a similar pattern: A person walking home at night would see a round blue light. This light—which was sometimes called a jack-o'-lantern or will-o'-the-wisp—was believed to be a puck carrying a lantern. By following the light, the puck's victim would be led into a pond, ditch, or marsh. The light would then disappear and laughing would be heard.

Although they did not usually cause serious harm, pucks showed that some fairies liked to cause mischief as their major source of fun.

But England was not the only country to have places named after fairies. Ireland also has "fairy hills," "fairy trees," and "fairy forts." Fairy forts are the ruins of ancient forts made from earth or stone. These forts were believed to be fairy dwellings, or portals to fairy realms. The Irish people treated these places with great caution. Fairies were said to sometimes shoot people with a dart called a "fairy blast," which could cause a blistering sore. Fairies could also give people a "fairy touch," which might cause sickness or mental illness. A "fairy path" was the route fairies took between their forts, which people were also cautious about.

Fairy fort in Ireland

Nisse

Described as a short old man with a white beard and red hat (sometimes called a gnome in other parts of Europe), a nisse was a Norwegian fairy. An animal lover, a nisse often lived in a house or barn and would help out with chores. A nisse was also mischievous and quick to anger, so people tried to stay on his good side. Anyone who harmed an animal would receive a sharp whack on their back from a nisse.

A nisse could be rewarded for his work with beer and porridge on special occasions, such as Christmas. The nisse is commonly thought to be the inspiration for Santa Claus.

In Ireland, encountering a fairy was something to avoid, as being whisked away to the fairy realm often led to a bad fate. Dawn and dusk were particularly dangerous times to be around a fairy fort or fairy path.

In Wales, fairies were also treated with caution and fear. To stop fairies from entering homes, Welsh people would hang iron tools on their walls. It was thought that iron would repel fairies.

People would not leave any fresh water sitting out. When outside, carrying bread in a pocket and wearing jackets inside out could confuse fairies and keep them away. One story told of a man traveling over Bedwellty Mountain, in Caerphilly County Borough, when fairies surrounded him. Some were dancing and others simply watched him closely. But when the man drew his iron hunting knife, the fairies vanished.

In Wales, fairies were said to dwell around trees, lakes, and also underground. But looking for fairies was not recommended. Few humans who were abducted to a fairy realm came back quite the same afterward. They were said to be "away with the fairies," a phrase used today to describe someone who is distracted, or out of touch with reality.

CHAPTER 4
Kings, Queens, and Fairy Realms

In British and Irish stories from the Middle Ages, fairies dwelled in forts, rings, human homes, and hidden realms that could be accessed through mysterious entryways called portals. So, what were these fairy realms like? According to a twelfth-century folktale, a twelve-year-old Welsh boy named Elidyr said he had visited such a place.

Elidyr was a lazy student who had skipped school to sit by a riverbank. Two tiny male fairies appeared and asked if he wanted to visit a place of fun, games, and tasty food. They took him through a tunnel to a warm green underground kingdom filled with blond-haired fairies. It was a world of riches, where there were no problems and no one ever lied, cheated, or stole. Elidyr became the playmate of the king's son and feasted on the fairies' milk-based food. He was even allowed to return home to visit his mother sometimes.

But when Elidyr's mother asked him to bring her some of the fairies' gold, he stole a magnificent gold ball. When he tried to take the gold ball through the tunnel to his mother, two angry fairies gave chase. When they got close, Elidyr dropped the gold ball. The fairies spat at Elidyr and went back through the tunnel, which closed behind them. Elidyr was never able to return to the fairy realm again.

In a similar folktale from this time, a British king called Herla was once visited by a small man claiming to be a fairy king. The fairy king asked if he could attend Herla's upcoming wedding, and then Herla could come to his. Herla agreed and the fairy spent three days at the king's wedding. A year later, the fairy king came to collect Herla and his attendants for his own wedding. They traveled through a tunnel to a magnificent underground castle lit by a magical light. Herla and his companions spent three days celebrating and left with many fine gifts, including horses, hounds, and hunting gear. But when they returned through the tunnel, they came across a woman who did not recognize Herla.

She said King Herla had disappeared two hundred years ago and had not been seen since. At this, Herla's attendants dismounted from their horses and immediately turned to dust. They were now

over two hundred years old and had been away from their home for two centuries! Herla, too fearful to dismount, was cursed to ride forever searching for his lost kingdom.

Patupaiarehe

Being taken to the realm of the patupaiarehe was a great fear of the New Zealand indigenous people known as the Maori. According to Maori folklore, the patupaiarehe built their fort-style homes deep in the forest and on misty mountaintops out of sight. The patupaiarehe were small, with reddish-gold hair

and eyes that ranged from light blue to black. They were unfriendly fairies who sometimes abducted people by luring them away with enchanting flute music. But humans could protect themselves by smearing the outside of their homes with shark oil. Cooking smells and open fires were also said to repel the patupaiarehe. As long as a fire was still glowing, people knew they were safe.

By the fourteenth century, fairies made their way into medieval romantic fiction—European tales about knights in armor on heroic quests. Some of these stories starred the legendary King Arthur and his Knights of the Round Table. In these tales, Arthur's own sister was Morgan le Fay, which means "Morgan the Fairy." Morgan, though, was a complicated character who caused Arthur's downfall and death. In the end, it was Morgan who took the dying Arthur on a boat to Avalon, where she ruled as queen of a fairy realm.

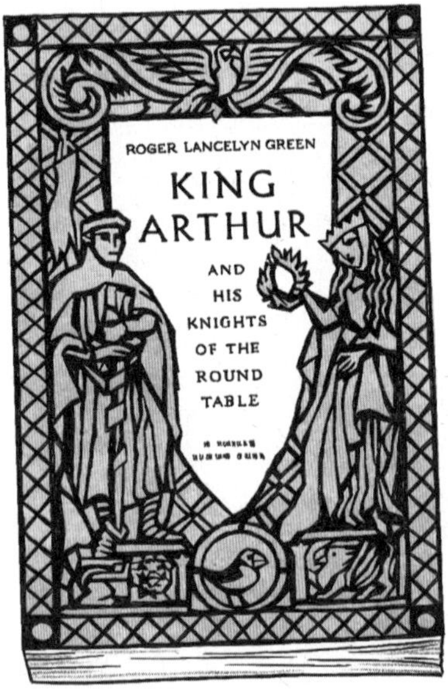

The fourteenth-century English author Geoffrey Chaucer wrote that during the days of King Arthur, "The isle of Britain was full of fairies."

Geoffrey Chaucer

But now, he said, they had been banished by Catholic priests. When England changed from a Catholic country to a Protestant one in the 1530s, ideas about fairies also began to change with the times.

In 1595, the English playwright William Shakespeare introduced audiences to the types of fairies that are familiar to us today. These were pretty fairies that played pranks on people but didn't cause lasting harm. Shakespeare's *A Midsummer Night's Dream* takes place in a wooded fairy realm where fairy king Oberon and queen Titania argue over a human changeling they are raising. Oberon asks his servant Puck to give Titania a potion so she will fall in love with the first living thing she sees after waking. This happens to be Bottom, a man with a donkey's head. In the end, Puck restores everything to normal and asks if the story was real or just a dream—like many reported fairy encounters.

William Shakespeare

Another famous Shakespearean fairy was Queen Mab from *Romeo and Juliet*. Mab is an important figure in the development of fairies. She is described as a tiny, mischievous fairy who manipulates people's dreams and braids the manes of horses at night. Mab also appears in poems of that time, including Ben Jonson's 1603 work "The Entertainment at Althorp." In the poem, Mab was said to spoil milk and make people fall into ponds and ditches. She could also steal babies.

Poets such as Ben Jonson were constantly trying to please the queen of England, Elizabeth I. They wanted to win favor and wealth. The poet Edmund Spenser had successfully achieved this aim with his 1589 poem, "The Faerie Queene"—a series of tales about knights in armor, including King Arthur, who perform heroic quests for the faerie queene. The noble, beautiful faerie queene represented Queen Elizabeth herself and Elizabeth was often called the "Faerie Queen" after Spenser's poem. Elizabeth awarded Spenser an annual salary of fifty British pounds for his work, a large amount in those days.

Queen Elizabeth I

The fairies of Shakespeare's, Jonson's, and Spenser's stories brought these authors great fame and rewards. But their fairies were no longer the dangerous, cruel, and unpredictable fairies of the Middle Ages. They had become the model for the modern fairies of today.

CHAPTER 5
Fairy Tales

Do fairies die? They do, according to seventeenth-century Scottish reverend Robert Kirk. Kirk said that he had studied fairies and interviewed people about fairy encounters for his 1692 book, *The Secret Commonwealth*. Kirk also said that fairies sometimes fought each other, which caused injury and even death. Although they lived longer than humans, fairies could die of old age. They even held their own funeral processions.

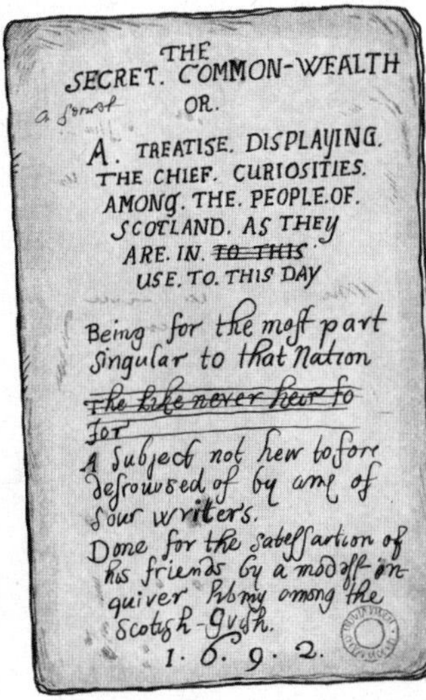

In 1800, English poet William Blake said

he had witnessed a fairy funeral procession. Blake was sitting in his garden in Sussex, England, when: "I heard a low and pleasant sound and I know not whence it came. At last I saw the broad leaf of a flower move and underneath I saw a procession of creatures, of the size and colour of green and grey grasshoppers, bearing a body laid out in a roseleaf, which they buried with songs and then disappeared. It was a fairy's funeral."

William Blake

Blake lived during a time when fairies were becoming even more popular in Britain than they had been during Shakespeare's time. But these fairies had more to do with Shakespeare's fairies than those who had come before. They were not scary, strange, or dangerous but small, cute, and mischievous. They had also grown wings.

Aziza

The Aziza are fairies from the folklore of the Benin people of West Africa. Small, with butterfly-type wings, the Aziza are one of the few examples of folklore fairies who can fly.

The Aziza were said to live in anthills and kapok trees and were helpful to humans. They showed people how to make fire and use plants as medicine. But when humans asked the Aziza for even more help, the fairies became upset and hid away in the deep forest. People say they are still there today and are much harder to see.

In the nineteenth century, Britain changed greatly due to the Industrial Revolution. Goods that were once made in people's homes were now manufactured in factories. Cities became crowded and polluted, and the sounds of clanging machines and factory smog filled the air.

The smog-filled air in London during the Industrial Revolution

"Romantic" artists, writers, and poets, such as William Blake, began to look back fondly at the past. The Romantics yearned for the quieter, cleaner past of Shakespeare's time. They imagined an ideal world, where life revolved around the green countryside and fairies might be seen flying around gardens.

Queen Victoria

The art of the Romantics shows how this popular view of fairies was becoming the new normal during the Victorian age (the years 1837–1901, named after Queen Victoria's reign). English artists like John Atkinson Grimshaw and John Anster Fitzgerald painted tiny fairies with delicate wings in rural settings. Fitzgerald was even called "Fairy Fitzgerald" for his work.

John Anster Fitzgerald painting *Cat Amongst Fairies*

Fairies in these artworks were more likely to be seen sheltering under tulips than sneaking through underground tunnels and stealing babies. They were magical miniature fairies sitting at tiny tables covered with rose petals at the end of gardens. They were, in other words, fairies designed to appeal to children.

Perhaps it is no surprise that children's stories featuring fairies became big sellers at this time. Some of these fairies starred in stories by the Brothers Grimm, Jacob and Wilhelm, in their 1812 book, *Children's and Household Tales*.

Jacob and Wilhelm Grimm

The Grimms based their stories on German folktales, many of which were about fairies. However, as new editions of their books were published, the Grimms began replacing the original fairies with different characters. In the Grimms' story "Rapunzel," for example, the fairy was turned into a wicked witch. In "Sleeping Beauty," the personality of the fairy was changed to be that of a wise woman. But despite these changes, these stories are still known to us today as fairy tales.

One of the most famous authors of fairy tales was Danish writer Hans Christian Andersen. His fairy tales were translated into many languages and still remain favorites today. One of Andersen's most famous fairy tales is "Thumbelina"—the story of a miniature girl who sprouts from a barleycorn and then becomes lost in the countryside. The story ends happily, though, as Thumbelina is taken to a sunny faraway land by a swallow and meets a flower-fairy prince. After marrying the prince, Thumbelina receives her own pair of fairy wings and the couple fly from flower to flower in their new life together. The art of many of these fairy tales showed fairies becoming cuter and more childlike.

Hans Christian Andersen

The tales themselves, however, had originally come from the folklore of different countries and were changed to suit Victorian-era styles and preferences.

Hans Christian Andersen's fairy tales were translated from Danish into English and became wildly popular in Britain, where local books about fairies were very much in-demand. These included the Fairy Books of Many Colors by Scottish author Andrew Lang and his wife,

Leonora Blanche Alleyne. This series of books took their stories from countries across Europe, America, China, Africa, the Middle East, and beyond. One of their most popular books was the 1889 *Blue Fairy Book*, which featured illustrated stories about fairies. The fairies in *The Blue Fairy Book* were, of course, winged.

By the end of the nineteenth century, wings had become to fairies what broomsticks are to witches, or fangs to vampires.

At the beginning of the twentieth century, the most famous winged fairy of all was about to be unveiled to the world. Tinker Bell is the fairy in *Peter Pan*, by Scottish playwright J.M. Barrie. *Peter Pan* is about a young boy who never grows up and flies away to have adventures in a magical realm called Neverland. It was written as a play and first performed in 1904 in the Duke of York's Theatre in London, England. In the play, Tinker Bell is the fairy folk's "tinker," that is someone who makes and mends pots and pans. But there is one part in the play where Tinker Bell is poisoned. Peter Pan tells the audience that Tinker Bell might survive if she knew children believed in fairies. He asks the audience: "Do you believe in fairies? Say quick that you believe! If you believe, clap your hands!"

J.M. Barrie

Before opening night, Barrie was nervous about this specific scene in the play. The audience would mainly be adults. If they didn't clap then the scene and perhaps the play would be a failure. The actress playing Peter Pan, Nina Boucicault, was nervous, too: "Suppose they don't clap? What do I do then?" she remembered asking. But she needn't have worried, as the audience stood up and clapped so loudly that Boucicault was reduced to tears. "I think everyone in the house believed in fairies!" she said afterward.

The play was a great success and made the character of Tinker Bell the world's best-known fairy. But *Peter Pan* had proven something else, too. Although fairies had now become cute characters from children's stories, adults could also enjoy them. No one, after all, is too old to believe in fairies.

Tian Xian Pei

China is another country that features flying fairies in its folklore. One famous story was that of “The Fairy Couple.” In this story, the seven fairy daughters of the all-powerful Jade Emperor flew down to Earth. While on Earth, the youngest daughter, Tian Xian Pei (say: TEE-en-shon-pay), fell in love with a farmer called Dong Yong, who was very poor and had many debts. To help him, the seven fairies wove ten pieces of precious silk for Dong Yong to sell and pay off his debts. But the Jade Emperor would not agree to the marriage and Tian Xian Pei was ordered to return home. Only on the seventh night of the seventh month was Tian Xian Pei allowed to fly to Earth to visit Dong Yong.

CHAPTER 6
Fairy Fever

Peter Pan the play ran for an astonishing ten years! During that time, many adults and children learned to clap their hands to show they believed in fairies. Belief in fairies increased. In fact, during the first two decades of the twentieth century, Britain became gripped by a sort of fairy fever.

Andrew Lang

This rise in fairy belief was helped along by the Fairy Books of Many Colors, by author Andrew Lang. Lang was a big believer in spirits and the unseen world. He was a president of the Society for Psychical (say: SIKE-ick-kul) Research, a group that examined ghosts, the paranormal, and supernatural beings such as fairies. The society attracted well-known people, including leading scientists, artists, and poets. Their work was part of a wider interest in "Spiritualism"—the idea that the spirit world was real and that humans could interact with it.

The Spiritualism movement had originated in the United States, but became popular in Britain during the early twentieth century. This was partly in reaction to the terrible events of World War I (1914–1918), when millions of young men lost their lives in the trenches of France and Belgium.

People looked for something more than the grim news of death and destruction in their daily lives. Spiritualism offered hope that there was some happiness beyond the physical world. Fairies—now seen as peaceful, friendly folk from the sunny green pastures of fairyland—fit in well with this hope.

Images were created to illustrate this new idea of fairies. Poster-size illustrations of fairies became big business. One such illustration was *The Piper of Dreams* by Estella Canziani, which showed a woodland man blowing a tin-whistle, surrounded by wispy, winged fairies. A staggering 250,000 prints of this illustration were sold in 1916 alone. But fairy art was not only for living-room walls: Fairy postcards were also available to buy and send to soldiers fighting in Europe. One artist producing these postcards was Cicely Mary Barker. Some of Barker's images were later printed in her 1923 book, *The Flower Fairies of the Spring*. The book showed tiny, winged fairies in flower gardens and became one of the most famous illustrated fairy books in the world. It also made sure winged fairies became an increasingly popular image.

While images of fairies appeared everywhere, there was no shortage of spiritualist groups insisting they were real. One such group was the Theosophical Society, led by Geoffrey Hodson. Hodson had written books about seeing fairies and given lectures on them. Skeptics,

Geoffrey Hodson

on the other hand, said there was absolutely no proof fairies existed. But then, at a 1919 Theosophical Society fairy lecture in Yorkshire, England, something remarkable happened. Polly Wright walked through the door apparently carrying evidence of fairies.

This evidence was, of course, the two fairy photos taken by Polly's daughter Elsie and her niece Frances. Polly could not have dreamed of the sensation the photos would cause. Nor could anyone have predicted that Arthur Conan Doyle would publish the photos as proof that fairies existed. Then, in Conan Doyle's 1920 and 1921 magazine articles, the fairy photos made headline news.

The photos were a big deal—not even the most dedicated fairy believers had dreamed of catching a real fairy on camera.

Not everyone believed the photos were real, though. Even Conan Doyle was unsure at first. The fairies did seem to have rather French-looking haircuts, someone suggested. An examination by the Eastman Kodak Company, which had manufactured the film, said the photos showed "no signs of being faked." However, Kodak would also not give the photos a stamp of authenticity. After his 1920 article, Conan Doyle asked Theosophical Society member Edward Gardner to visit Elsie and Frances. Gardner asked the girls to take three more photos of fairies, which they did. Geoffrey Hodson also visited the girls and reported he had seen live fairies all around them. This was enough for Conan Doyle to confirm the photos were not hoaxes and publish his 1922 book, *The Coming of the Fairies*.

Arthur Conan Doyle (1859–1930)

Born in Edinburgh, Scotland, Arthur Conan Doyle developed the idea for his Sherlock Holmes detective character while attending medical school. He liked the idea of a detective solving a crime in the same logical way a doctor would diagnose a patient's illness. Sherlock Holmes first appeared in the 1887 novel *A Study in Scarlet* and went on to star in fifty-nine more stories, making Conan Doyle a world-famous author.

Arthur Conan Doyle also worked as a war correspondent and ran a military hospital before becoming involved in the Spiritualism movement. He believed in fairies and the paranormal. After his death, thousands joined a séance in London to try to contact the departed author.

Debate about the Cottingley fairy photos raged for decades. Spiritualists insisted they were real, while nonbelievers said they were fake. People in both groups wanted to know more. In 1927, the Fairy Investigation Society was created by British army captain Sir Quentin Craufurd. Its purpose was to investigate and collect information about fairies. Members did have to believe in fairies to join the society, though.

Meanwhile, Conan Doyle's articles had captured attention as far away as Australia, South Africa, and North America. During the nineteenth and twentieth centuries, millions of Europeans had sailed across the Atlantic Ocean to start new lives in North America. Some said that fairies had stowed away on the ships from Europe with them. Many British and Irish people had settled in Canada's Atlantic provinces.

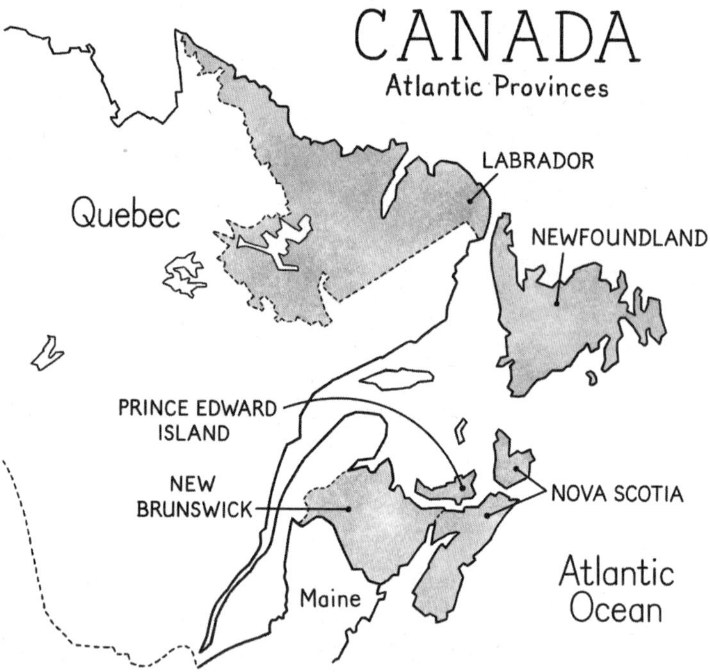

Here, they reported fairy encounters that were often scary. Canadian fairies were said to shine lights to wreck incoming ships, haunt houses, and even attack people. In the provinces of Newfoundland and Labrador, people reported seeing groups of fairies dancing, fairies braiding horses' manes in barns, and abducting people. In the 1960s, there was at least one report of a baby being replaced with a fairy changeling.

Fairy sightings were also reported in the United States. One fairy encounter occurred in 1956, in Derry, New Hampshire. Here, Alfred Horne was cutting down Christmas trees when he saw a strange creature in front of him. It was green, two feet tall, with two holes for a nose and floppy ears like an elephant. After looking at the creature for several minutes, Horne grabbed it by the leg. But the creature made such a blood-curdling scream that Horne dropped it. Horne was later told he had met a Pukwudgie—

an ancient fairy from Native American folklore. Pukwudgies were knee-high forest dwellers who played pranks on travelers and sometimes stole human children.

There were many similarities between the folktale fairies of North America and Europe. But in North America, an already famous fairy was about to become a movie superstar: Tinker Bell. In 1953, Disney released the animated film *Peter Pan*, with Tinker Bell as a central character. Walt Disney himself had joined the Fairy Investigation Society in the 1950s and had studied Irish fairies. After the film *Peter Pan* became a smash hit, Disney made Tinker Bell a company mascot. A whole Disney Fairy franchise of movies, comics, video games, and books would follow. The winged Tinker Bell was soon flying across the screen sprinkling fairy dust at the start of Disney movies—the fairy had become a true movie star.

In many ways, Disney's Tinker Bell had followed the popular image of fairies created by Shakespeare, the Romantics, Cicely Mary Barker's illustrations, and the Cottingley photos. The image of the friendly, fluttering, flower-loving fairy seemed to be here to stay.

Then, in 1983, shocking fairy news rocked the world. An investigation by the *British Journal of Photography* concluded that the Cottingley fairy photos had been faked. For nearly seventy years, Elsie and Frances had insisted that the photos were genuine. But after the *British Journal of Photography* investigation, the women admitted the photos had been a hoax the whole time.

The girls had cut out pictures from a 1914 book called *Princess Mary's Gift Book* and glued wings to them. They had then attached the pictures to the bushes with hatpins so they could take their photos with them. Elsie said that what had started as a prank became more serious after Arthur Conan Doyle became involved:

"Two village kids and a brilliant man like Conan Doyle—well, we could only keep quiet," she said.

"It was just Elsie and I having a bit of fun," Frances added. "I can't understand to this day why people were taken in. They wanted to be taken in."

Jogah

There are many fairies in Native American folklore. The Iroquois believe in tiny fairies called Jogah, or the "little people." The Jogah were said to live underground and were only visible to children. In one Jogah story, a girl escaped her cruel aunt

and uncle and was discovered by a group of Jogah in a cornfield. They gave her winged moccasins and flew her to a fairy realm. After the girl feasted with the Jogah, they returned her to her aunt and uncle. But first, the Jogah sent a pack of wolves to eat everything in the house. Afterward, the aunt and uncle were kind to the girl.

CHAPTER 7
Fairies Today

The confession of Frances and Elsie ended the greatest fairy hoax of all time. But it didn't stop the photos becoming one of the most recognized images of fairies in the twentieth century. Before then, people had reported seeing fairies for thousands of years. They were often dangerous and easily offended. The fairies of folklore stole children, abducted adults, and sometimes attacked people. They didn't have wings. But over time, the image of fairies changed. They became miniature, winged, playful, and friendly. No wonder so many people believed in the Cottingley photos, which showed delicate fairies dancing joyously around schoolgirls.

Although the Cottingley photos were found

to be fakes, people's interest in fairies has only increased since. Fairies have played a starring role in modern popular culture from the moment Disney made Tinker Bell a company mascot. Today, fairies appear across film, television, comic books, graphic novels, books, and video games. In the 1980s, *The Legend of Zelda* video game introduced the Great Fairies as main characters.

The game's later character Navi is perhaps one of the most familiar gaming fairies of all time. Fairies also make an appearance in recent films, such as *Rise of the Guardians* (2012), *Cinderella* (2015), *Maleficent* (2014), and

Maleficent: Mistress of Evil (2019). Based on the 1697 fairy story "Sleeping Beauty," the Maleficent movies feature both good and bad fairies, and star Angelina Jolie as a dark fey, a fairy who is set on revenge.

There are also fairies in television shows around the world. These shows include Italy's *PopPixie*, China's *The Little Fairy*, and Australia's *The Fairies*. But fairy shows are not only for children.

In 2017, a series of fairy YouTube videos produced by Erwin Saunders became a viral sensation. Saunders is an eccentric white-bearded British man who wears rubber boots and bumbles around looking for fairies in the English woodlands. Saunders says he has been searching for fairies for twenty-five years, and in the videos, real fairies are seen (with the help of special effects).

Although many people are only aware of fairies from their role in popular culture, actual fairy sightings are also on the rise. Authors have been recording people's fairy encounters for centuries. In the 1996 book *Seeing Fairies*, author Marjorie Johnson reported fairy sightings from around the world. An even larger worldwide survey of fairy encounters was taken in the three-volume *Fairy Census* by S. R. Young. Part 1 covers Britain and Ireland, Part 2, the United States, and Part 3, Europe, Australia, and the rest of the world.

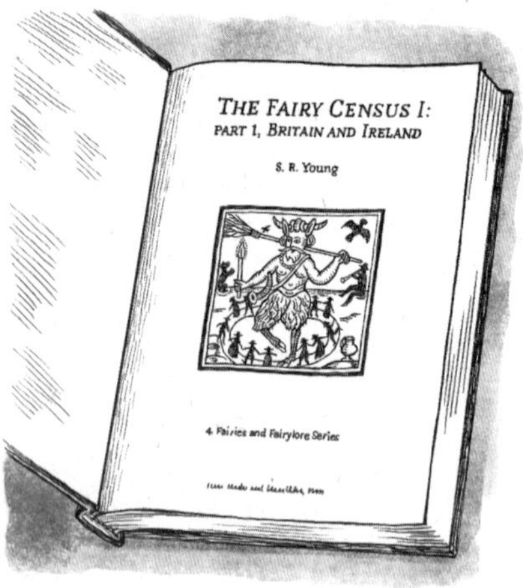

The censuses reported fairy encounters that people had recorded on an online database. There are also groups that investigate fairies, including the Fairy Investigation Society, which is still going strong since its founding in 1927. Membership in the society is free, although believing in fairies is no longer a requirement.

Today in the United Kingdom, where so much of what we know about fairies comes from, there are modern fairy festivals and fairs. These include music, theater, storytelling, and stalls selling fairy goods. Talks and workshops at these events explore the mysterious world of fairies and help people prepare to see fairies themselves.

This can be easier said than done. Hundreds of years ago, humans spent most of their time outside, working on the land. There was not the constant sound of traffic, telephones, or planes flying overhead. In this quieter world it may have been easier to be ready to see a fairy. However, many still believe it is possible today.

Maybe you have seen a fairy yourself? Perhaps in a calm forest or field, the air around you felt different, and there was a sensation of being watched. There may have been the faint sound of music, or laughter. Maybe you noticed a tiny figure out of the corner of your eye, or something strange scamper away? Why not try looking out the next time you are in a natural setting? Who knows—if you are quiet and still, maybe a fairy will find you.

Timeline of Fairies

700 BCE	Early mentions of fairies in Homer's *Iliad* and *Odyssey*
1188 CE	Welsh priest Gerald of Wales writes about fairy folktales and encounters, including the story of Elidyr
1589	English poet Edmund Spenser writes "The Faerie Queene," dedicated to Queen Elizabeth I
1595	Playwright William Shakespeare introduces fairy characters in *A Midsummer Night's Dream*
1603	English poet Ben Jonson writes about the fairy Queen Mab in *The Entertainment at Althorp*
1692	Scottish reverend Robert Kirk writes a book about fairies called *The Secret Commonwealth*
1889	Scottish author Andrew Lang and his wife Leonora Blanche Alleyne publish the *Blue Fairy Book*
1904	Scottish playwright J.M. Barrie's play *Peter Pan*, which features the fairy character Tinker Bell, is first performed in London, England
1917	Nine-year-old Frances Griffith and sixteen-year-old Elsie Wright produce two photos of fairies, in Cottingley, Yorkshire, England
1953	Walt Disney releases an animated film of *Peter Pan*
2023	Three-volume *Fairy Census* publishes a list of fairy encounters from around the world

Timeline of the World

7000 BCE	Maize (corn) becomes a staple food for the early people of southern Mexico
1589 CE	The Battle of Suriagehara takes place between warring Japanese samurai clans
1595	Mehmed III begins his nine-year rule as sultan of the Ottoman Empire
1603	Za Sellase removes Yaqob as emperor of Ethiopia and appoints his cousin Za Dengel in his place
1692	Three women are charged with witchcraft as the Salem witch trials begin in Salem Village, Massachusetts Bay Colony
1889	Eiffel Tower opens in Paris, France, the tallest structure in the world at 984 feet at the time
1904	International Alliance of Women to promote women's equality and gender rights is founded
1923	Mount Etna in Sicily, Italy, erupts, destroying the village of Mascali and leaving tens of thousands of people homeless
1953	New Zealander Edmund Hillary and Nepalese Tenzing Norgay become the first people to reach the top of Mount Everest, the highest mountain in the world
2023	Spain beats England 1–0 in the final of the FIFA Women's World Cup soccer competition

Bibliography

***Books for young readers**

*Claybourne, Anna. ***The Fairy Atlas: Fairy Folk of the World***. London: Laurence King Publishing, 2022.

Cotterell, Arthur. ***Mythology of the World***. London: Anness Publishing, 2023.

Evans-Wentz, W. Y. ***The Fairy-Faith in Celtic Countries***. Delhi: JollyJoy Books Pvt Ltd, 2024.

*Hawkins, Emily. ***A Natural History of Fairies***. London: Frances Lincoln Children's Books, 2020.

Kirk, Robert. ***The Secret Commonwealth of Elves, Fauns and Fairies***. Delhi: JollyJoy Books Pvt Ltd, 2024.

Purkiss, Diane. ***Fairies and Fairy Stories: A History***. Gloucestershire: Tempus, 2007.

Sugg, Richard. ***Fairies: A Dangerous History***. London: Reaktion Books, 2019.

Yeats, W. B. ***Irish Fairy and Folk Tales***. Delhi: Grapevine India Publishers, 2023.

Young, Simon. ***Magical Folk: British and Irish Fairies—500 AD to the Present***. London: Gibson Square, 2017.